Bored Bella

Learns About Fiction and Nonfiction

by Sandy Donovan
illustrated by Leeza Hernandez

PICTURE WINDOW BOOKS
a capstone imprint

Thanks to our advisers for their expertise, research, and advice:

Diane R. Chen, Library Information Specialist
John F. Kennedy Middle School, Nashville, Tennessee

Terry Flaherty, Ph.D., Professor of English
Minnesota State University, Mankato

Editors: Shelly Lyons and Jennifer Besel
Designer: Abbey Fitzgerald
Art Director: Nathan Gassman
Production Specialist: Jane Klenk
The illustrations in this book were created with pencil, acrylics, collage, and digital mixed-media.

Photo Credits: Capstone Studio/Karon Dubke, 4 (bottom); Corbis/Royalty-Free, 4 (top right); Digital Vision (Getty Images), 4 (top left)

Picture Window Books
151 Good Counsel Drive
P.O. Box 669
Mankato, MN 56002-0669
877-845-8392
www.picturewindowbooks.com

Printed in the United States of America in North Mankato, Minnesota.
092009
005618CGS10

 All books published by Picture Window Books are manufactured with paper containing at least 10 percent post-consumer waste.

Library of Congress Cataloging-in-Publication Data
Donovan, Sandra, 1967-
Bored Bella learns about fiction and nonfiction / by Sandy Donovan; illustrated by Leeza Hernandez.
p. cm. — (In the library)
Includes index.
ISBN 978-1-4048-5758-2 (library binding)
ISBN 978-1-4048-6105-3 (paperback)
1. Literary form—Juvenile literature. I. Hernandez, Leeza. II. Title.
PN45.5.D66 2010
808.3071—dc22   2009030403

This is Bored Bella. She is always bored. Bored, bored, bored. Snoozaroo. Everything is boring to Bored Bella.

One day, Bella's class went to the library to check out books.

"Ho, hum,"
thought Bella.
"Books are boring."

IN THE LIBRARY

3

The librarian's name was Ms. Paige Turner. Bella thought Ms. Turner was kind of . . . interesting. But just a little.

She asked the kids what they'd like to read about. Jamal said he would like to read about **sharks**, and Lacy wanted to read about **soccer**. Janet said she would like to read about **outer space**.

Bored Bella didn't want to read about anything. She just sat there, looking bored.

"Once you know what you want to read about, you can decide if you want to read **fiction** or **nonfiction**," said Ms. Turner. "Both kinds of books can be very interesting."

"What does 'fish king' mean?" asked Lacy. She thought it had to do with sharks.

Fiction, said Ms. Turner. "Fiction is a story made up by an author."

"Authors sometimes write fiction so the action in the story sounds like it really happened." Ms. Turner continued. "In this book, it says, 'Once there was a space pirate named Gerald.' But we know space pirates aren't real."

7

"So what's nonfiction?" asked Jamal.

"I'm glad you asked," said Ms. Turner, putting on a space helmet. "The goal of nonfiction is to give information. Authors write nonfiction books to give facts about real people, places, or things. People read nonfiction to learn about something."

READ!

HOW TO PLAY SOCCER

"The author might write, 'People sent a robot to Mars. The robot explored the planet.' That's a pretty awesome story, so you might think it's made up," said Ms. Turner. "But this is nonfiction, so it's true. People do send robots to Mars. They're called Mars rovers."

Bella thought Mars rovers sounded kind of interesting. **But she didn't admit it.**

Ms. Turner said, "In fiction, the author invents people to be in the story. These people are called characters. The characters usually have a problem. **They do their best to solve it.**"

Ms. Turner continued,

"Here's an example:

'Space pirate Gerald was lost.
He wanted to go home.'
Gerald the space pirate is a
made-up character."

Characters don't have to be people. They can be animals, robots, or imaginary creatures, such as monsters or space aliens.

"So if it's a story, it's **fiction**," said Lacy.

"Not always," Ms. Turner replied. **"Nonfiction** can be told like a story. But the information is true."

"You can read the story of how a Mars rover was launched into space and what it did once it got to Mars," she said.

"You can even read nonfiction stories about people, such as the people who built the rovers," said Ms. Turner.

Nonfiction stories about people are called biographies.

"I like fiction best," said Janet. "Everything in fiction is made up. **That's cool.**"

Ms. Turner raised a finger in the air. "Actually," she said, "even though **fiction is made up**, it can have real facts in it. But if the author's goal was to tell a made-up story, then the book is fiction."

ROVER RD.

BLACK HOLE BOULEVARD

SPACE MAP

"Here's an example: 'A rover rolled across Mars.' This part is true. 'A space pirate named Gerald landed nearby to ask the rover for directions,'" she said.

"The part about the space pirate Gerald is **made up**," Ms. Turner said. "This story is fiction, but it has a **true detail** about the **Mars rover** in it."

Bella raised her hand. She did it in a very bored-looking way. But secretly she was interested.

"I like books with drawings," she said when Ms. Turner called on her. "Um, I mean, some people, if they are not totally bored, might like books with drawings in them. So should those people get fiction or nonfiction?"

"Either one!" exclaimed Ms. Turner. "Both fiction and nonfiction books can have illustrations, or drawings."

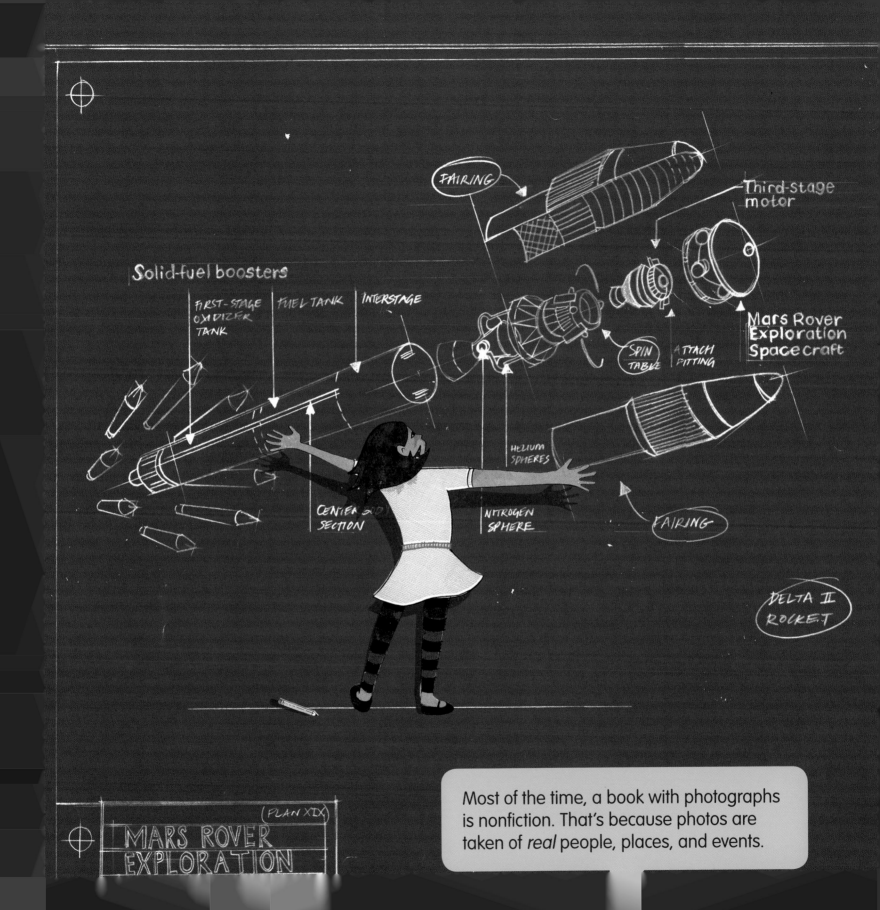

Most of the time, a book with photographs is nonfiction. That's because photos are taken of *real* people, places, and events.

"How can you tell if a book is fiction or nonfiction?"

asked Bella. "By the title?"

"Good question," replied Ms. Turner.

"You can't tell by the title," she said. "Look here. These two books are both called *Mars Adventure*. But this one is fiction, and the other is nonfiction."

"That's no help," said Bella.

"Well, here's a hint," said Ms. Turner.

"Fiction and nonfiction books are shelved in different parts of the library."

"Here's another hint," Ms. Turner said.

"Library books have call numbers on their spines."

If the book is fiction, the call number starts with *F* or *Fic*. That stands for 'fiction.' Below that is the first letter or first few letters of the author's last name."

"A great read for bedtime."

Fic
Gis

$15.00 USD

MARS ADVENTURE

Fic
Gis

MARS ADVENTURE

523.43
Hen

"If the book is nonfiction, it has a **Dewey** call number," Ms. Turner continued. "The call number has three digits, then a period, or decimal point. Then it has more numbers after the period. Below the call numbers are the first three letters of the author's last name.

n of astronauts

top scientists

de amazing and cool

scoveries sending Mars

vers to the Red Planet.

523.43

Hen

Workers at the Library of Congress in Washington, D.C., look at newly published books. They label the books fiction or nonfiction. They also give nonfiction books their Dewey call numbers.

"There's another way to tell if a book is fiction or nonfiction," said Ms. Turner. "Read the description of the book on the back cover or inside flap. When you read it, ask yourself:

- What is the book about? What happens in the book?

- Is the purpose of the book to give information or tell a story?"

"If the book is about Mars rovers and it gives details about them, it's probably nonfiction. If the book is about a made-up character who lands near a Mars rover, it's fiction." Ms. Turner looked at all the kids. "Any questions?" she asked.

"Yes," said Bella.

"Can we check out books now?"

Glossary

call number—the series of numbers and letters that tell where a book is located in a library; call numbers always start with one of the 10 hundreds groups.

characters—the people in a story

fiction—something that is made up or untrue; fiction books are usually stories.

information—facts or knowledge

nonfiction—something that is true; nonfiction books give information for readers to learn.

spine—the part of a book's cover that's on the edge; pages are attached to the inside of the spine, and information about the book is printed on the outside.

More Books to Read

Berg, Brook. *What Marion Taught Willis.* Fort Atkinson, Wis.: Upstart Books, 2005.

Buzzeo, Toni. *Our Librarian Won't Tell Us Anything!* Fort Atkinson, Wis.: Upstart Books, 2006.

Morris, Carla D. *The Boy Who Was Raised by Librarians.* Atlanta: Peachtree, 2007.

Thompson, Carol. *Mr. Wiggle Loves to Read.* Columbus, Ohio: Waterbird Books, 2003.

Internet Sites

FactHound offers a safe, fun way to find Internet sites related to this book. All of the sites on FactHound have been researched by our staff.

Here's all you do:

Visit *www.facthound.com*

FactHound will fetch the best sites for you!

www.FactHound.com

23

Index

Stage 2 Ignition
t = 4 min. 30.9 sec
Alt = 118.9 km (73.9 mi)
VI = 22.326 km/h (13.973 mph)

Stage 2 Cutoff #1
t = 9 min. 35.5 sec.
Alt = 170.4 km (105.9 mi)
VI = 28.085 km/h (17.467 mph)

Booster Jettison (3)
t = 2 min. 11.8 sec
Alt = 52.4 km (32.6 mi)
VI = 9.046 km/h (5.821 mph)

Look for all of the books in the In the Library series:

* Bob the Alien Discovers the Dewey Decimal System

* Bored Bella Learns About Fiction and Nonfiction

* Karl and Carolina Uncover the Parts of a Book

* Pingpong Perry Experiences How a Book Is Made

LIFT OFF

BOOSTER IMPACT

BOOSTER IMPACT

LAUNCH PHASES

Numbers approximate for first day of ROVER launch period.

(00.12A)

24